Donating

DONATIONS
Clothes

...ATIONS
...ooks

DONATIONS
Toys

Children's Community School
14702 Sylvan Street
Van Nuys, CA 91411
818-780-6226

Published in the United States of America by Cherry Lake Publishing
Ann Arbor, Michigan
www.cherrylakepublishing.com

Content Adviser: Danielle Peart, CPA
Reading Adviser: Cecilia Minden, PhD, Literacy expert and children's author
Book Design: Jennifer Wahi
Illustrator: Jeff Bane

Photo Credits: © Roman Stetsyk/Shutterstock.com, 5; © Kajohnwit Boonsom/Shutterstock.com, 7; © wavebreakmedia/Shutterstock.com, 9; © Mila Supinskaya Glashchenko/Shutterstock.com, 11; © Titikul_B/Shutterstock.com, 13; © Victoria 1/Shutterstock.com, 15; © michaeljung/Shutterstock.com, 17; © Africa Studio/Shutterstock.com, 19; © Rawpixel.com/Shutterstock.com, 21; © mangostock/Shutterstock.com, 23; Cover, 1, 6, 10, 14, Jeff Bane

Library of Congress Cataloging-in-Publication Data

Names: Colby, Jennifer, 1971- author.
Title: Donating / Jennifer Colby.
Description: Ann Arbor : Cherry Lake Publishing, [2018] | Series: My guide to money | Includes bibliographical references and index.
Identifiers: LCCN 2018003326| ISBN 9781534128996 (hardcover) | ISBN 9781534130692 (pdf) | ISBN 9781534132191 (pbk.) | ISBN 9781534133891 (hosted ebook)
Subjects: LCSH: Charities--Juvenile literature. | Charitable uses, trusts, and foundations--Juvenile literature.
Classification: LCC HV48 .C65 2018 | DDC 361.7/4--dc23
LC record available at https://lccn.loc.gov/2018003326

Printed in the United States of America
Corporate Graphics

About the author: Jennifer Colby is a school librarian in Michigan. She donates her time and money to causes she believes in.

About the illustrator: Jeff Bane and his two business partners own a studio along the American River in Folsom, California, home of the 1849 Gold Rush. When Jeff's not sketching or illustrating for clients, he's either swimming or kayaking in the river to relax.

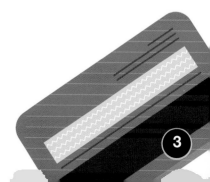

Have you given something away? That is donating!

We donate to help others.

Many people need help.
There are many different
ways to help them.

Where else can you volunteer?

You can donate time.
This is **volunteering**.
People volunteer to help animals.
They volunteer at **soup kitchens**.

You can donate money. It will go to **charities**.

What else can you donate?

You can donate goods.
Goods can be clothes or toys.
Goods can also be food.

Many groups ask for donations.
They support a **cause**. They
want to help others.

Some people plan a **donation drive**.

They raise money. They gather goods. They get people to notice problems. They ask for volunteers.

Ask how you can help others. Can you start a donation drive? Can you help raise money for a cause? Ask your teacher!

glossary

cause (KAWZ) something important that a group supports

charities (CHAR-ih-teez) groups that help people who need things

donation drive (doh-NAY-shuhn DRIVE) an effort to collect things to help others

soup kitchens (SOOP KICH-enz) places where poor and homeless people can eat for free

volunteering (vol-uhn-TEER-ing) doing work without being forced to or getting paid for it

index